Polar Bears

Written by Lee Wang

Flying Start
to Literacy®

Contents

What are polar bears?

Polar bears are the largest bears in
the world. They can grow to over
one metre tall, over three metres long
and can weigh more than 700 kilograms.

Polar bears are mammals that have fur
on their bodies. They give birth to cubs.

Polar bears live in the frozen northern
parts of the world. They hunt on the
sea ice on the edge of the land.

4

How do polar bears keep warm?

Polar bears have fur, skin and a layer of fat to help keep them warm.

A polar bear's fur looks white, but each hair has no colour. Each hair is a clear, hollow tube. These tubes allow the sun's energy to go directly to the bear's skin, which helps it to keep warm.

A polar bear's skin is black under its fur. Black is a good colour for soaking up heat.

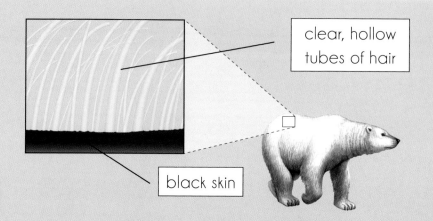

clear, hollow tubes of hair

black skin

A polar bear has a layer of fat that keeps it warm in the freezing water.

If a polar bear's fur stayed wet for too long, the polar bear would get very cold. When a polar bear comes out of the water, it shakes water from its fur. A polar bear can also squeeze water from its fur by dragging itself across the ice.

How do polar bears move?

On the sea ice

Polar bears can run fast on the sea ice. They can jump from one patch of sea ice to another. This is because they have pads on the soles of their feet and they also have long hairs between their toes that help them grip the ice.

Polar bears can move across the ice without slipping.

In the water

Polar bears also spend time in water.
They use their front paws to swim.
They have webbing between the toes
of their front paws. This helps them
to swim quickly in the water.

They can swim as fast as ten kilometres
per hour and they can swim very
long distances.

What do polar bears eat?

Polar bears eat other animals. They mainly eat seals that swim under the sea ice. They also eat small mammals, sea birds and fish.

Polar bears need to eat a lot of food to stay alive and to build up a thick fat layer to keep them warm.

Hunting

When polar bears are hunting, their white coat helps them to blend in with the ice and this makes it hard for other animals to see them.

Polar bears can smell seals through the ice. To catch the seals, they dig in the ice to make a hole. As a seal swims by, the polar bear uses its sharp claws to pounce on the seal and drag it up through the hole.

How do polar bears care for their young?

At the start of winter, female polar bears dig a warm, safe den in the snow. Their cubs are born in the den. These cubs are tiny and blind at birth, but they grow quickly. The mother feeds her cubs milk from her body.

The mother and
her cubs come out
of the den in spring.
The cubs stay with
their mother for
at least two years.

Are polar bears dangerous?

Polar bears are dangerous wild animals. In their natural habitat polar bears stay away from people. But polar bears sometimes wander into towns to look for food.

When polar bears come into towns, rangers make loud noises to scare the polar bears away. If this doesn't work the rangers tranquillise the polar bears and return them safely to their natural habitat.

Are polar bears in danger?

Polar bears are in danger because it is getting harder for them to hunt for food. This is because the sea ice is melting and the polar bears have to swim further to find their food. Some polar bears swim so far from land that they cannot get back to land.

If female polar bears do not find enough food they cannot feed their cubs and they will not survive.

Glossary

den   a cave that an animal can shelter in

mammal   a warm-blooded animal that makes milk to feed its young

pad   a soft part on the bottom of an animal's foot

prey   an animal that is hunted for food

tranquillise   to put an animal to sleep

webbing   folds of skin that join an animal's toes to each other